MARGARET BRANDMAN

JUNIOR TRAX

Illustrations by Don Ezard
Edited by – Mark Bradbury and Margaret Brandman
Page layout by David Parker

Exclusive distributors for Australia and New Zealand
Encore Music Distributors
227 Napier St, Fitzroy VIC 3065 Australia
Phone +61 3 9415 6677
Facsimile +61 3 9415 6655
Email sales@encoremusic.com.au

This book © Copyright 2015 by Margaret Brandman trading as Jazzem Music
46 Gerrale St, Cronulla NSW 2230 Australia
ISBN 978-0-949683-50-2
ISMN 970-0-720010-25-0
ORDER NUMBER MMP 8001
International copyright secured (APRA/AMCOS). All rights reserved.

Unauthorised reproduction of any part of this publication by any means,
including photocopying, is an infringement of copyright.

Introduction

The material in this book is designed as performance repertoire for the transition period between the *Junior Primer* and *Contemporary Piano Method Level 1A*. The skills introduced in the primer are expanded and applied to well-known tunes.

Educational features

- The tunes are presented in gently graded sequence
- All tunes are in easy keys (C major, G major and A natural minor)
- First section – uses only whole notes, half notes, dotted half notes and quarter notes
- Latter section of book – introduces eighth notes
- The arrangements provide practice in two-part playing using mostly continuous lines in both parts so as not to disturb the reading and to develop security on the instrument
- The arrangements are designed to continue the direction-reading skills introduced in the *Junior Primer*
- Duet parts are included for ensemble experience and to provide a variety of music reading skills
- Suitable for small hands as most tunes are in one hand position and use intervals up to a fifth; although the interval of an octave is occasionally used for effect
- Many of the arrangements are suitable for transposition
- Lyrics are included *above* the treble staff so as not to disturb the pattern and direction reading between the staves
- New skills introduced at this level include –
  a) Playing tunes with varying intervals in each hand
  b) Playing longer note values in one hand and shorter note values in the other
  c) Slight changes in hand position
- 'Slip finger' changes on one note are indicated by a dash before the finger number
  For instance, -3 means change over to the third finger after sounding the note
  This could be short for 4-3
- The page references for the connection of materials with *Contemporary Piano Method Book 1A* or *Daily Dexter-Flexers* are indicated in the final column in the chart on page 4

For more information on the methodology refer to my website: **www.margaretbrandman.com**

I hope these easy arrangements of familiar tunes provide the beginning pianist with many hours of enjoyment while learning valuable pianistic skills !

Margaret Brandman
PhD.Mus/Arts., F.Mus.Ed ASMC., F.Comp. ASMC., B.Mus.,(Syd)
T.Mus.A., L.Perf. ASMC., A.Mus.A., Hon.FNMSM. (UK)

International Woman of the Year for Music (2003)
awarded by the International Biographic Centre - Cambridge, England

Contents

Fantastic Finger-Flexers	5
Twinkle, Twinkle Little Star	6
I am a Fine Musician	7
More Finger-Flexers	8
Come Clap Your Hands	9
London Bridge is Falling Down	10
Two Fat Gentlemen	11
Scooting, Riding, Skating	12
I Love Little Pussy	14
Little Bo Peep	15
Warm Kitty, Soft Kitty	16
Jingle Jangle	17
Five Little Ducks	18
Mister Frog	19
The Jumping Flea	20
Said the Kind Kangaroo	22
Hush-a-bye, Don't You Cry	23
Award Certificate	24
Duet parts	25 - 32

Piano/keyboard skills you can learn while having fun!

Song	Feature	Skill	Time Signature	Key	Page	CPM 1A
Fantastic Finger-Flexers 1, 2 and 3	Hands together Step & Skip mixtures	Play varying intervals in each hand	4/4	C	5	Use with p19-21
Twinkle, Twinkle Little Star	Stepping patterns	LH sustains ½ notes, while RH plays ¼ notes	4/4	C	6	22
I am a Fine Musician	Skipping patterns, harmonic steps and skips and introduction of C triad	LH sustains ½ notes, while RH plays ¼ notes	4/4 Anacrusis	C	7	22
More Finger-Flexers 4 & 5	Hands together Skip-Plus-Ones & Jumps	Counterpoint skills Quarter and half note mixtures	4/4	C Am	8	23
Come Clap Your Hands	4ths and 5ths included in melody	¼ rests on the first beat of the bar, independent left and right hand lines	4/4	C	9	24
London Bridge is Falling Down	More 4ths	Two-part playing The octave leap	4/4	C	10	25
Two Fat Gentlemen	Repeated notes, and Jumps plus the tie	Harmonic steps, Finger changes	3/4	C	11	29
Scooting, Riding, Skating	Left hand features repetitive, 3rds, 4ths, and 5ths	Use of ties to create *syncopation*	4/4	C	12	30
I Love Little Pussy	Left hand rhythm ♩ ♩ against RH continuous quarter notes ♩♩♩	Detached repeated notes in one hand, while playing legato intervals in the other	3/4 Anacrusis	G	14	31
Little Bo Peep	Triads and harmonic 3rds	Strengthen the fingers to play chords	3/4	G	15	34
Warm Kitty	Left hand harmonic thirds moving by steps	Build your technique for doubled thirds	4/4	C	16	35
Jingle Jangle	Harmonic intervals – steps through jumps	Read across the page to connect similar and different notes	4/4	C	17	DDF Gp2&3
Five Little Ducks	Two treble staves, Eighth notes, repeat sign	Rhythm skills with eighths	4/4	C	18	DDF Gp2&3
Mister Frog	Eighth notes and dotted quarter notes Pause sign	Fermata	4/4 Anacrusis	C	19	DDF Gp2&3
Jumping Flea	Melody in both RH (first half), melody in LH, with counter melody, in second half of tune	Eighth notes, hand-position change	4/4 Anacrusis	C	20	DDF Gp2&3
Said the Kind Kangaroo	Hand position changes	Introduction of the *sharp*	3/4 Anacrusis	C	22	DDF Gp2&3
Hush-a-bye, Don't You Cry	Arranged with parallel 5ths for 'Indian' effect Dotted ¼ note rhythm	Melody travelling from hand to hand – reading intervals across the middle of the Great Staff	4/4	Am nat/ Aeolian	23	DDF Gp2&3

Magic Reading Page
Fantastic Finger-Flexers
Hands together using different intervals!

* First play each of these finger-flexers separately
* Finger trace the music before playing hands together
* When playing hands together, read the **bass part** first
* Prepare the left hand interval by poising the finger above the key, then do the same with the right hand interval
* When ready, depress both keys at the same time

Finger-Flexer No.1

Margaret Brandman

Play slowly

Finger-Flexer No.2
Steps and Skips
Rubbing *tummy* - patting *head*!

Margaret Brandman

Say the directions as you play!

Finger-Flexer No.3
Steps and Skips
Rubbing *head* - patting *tummy*!

Margaret Brandman

Copyright © 2015 Margaret Brandman
International copyright secured APRA/AMCOS. All rights reserved
Photocopying is illegal

Twinkle Twinkle Little Star

Traditional

See duet page 1

Arrangement by Margaret Brandman

Moderato

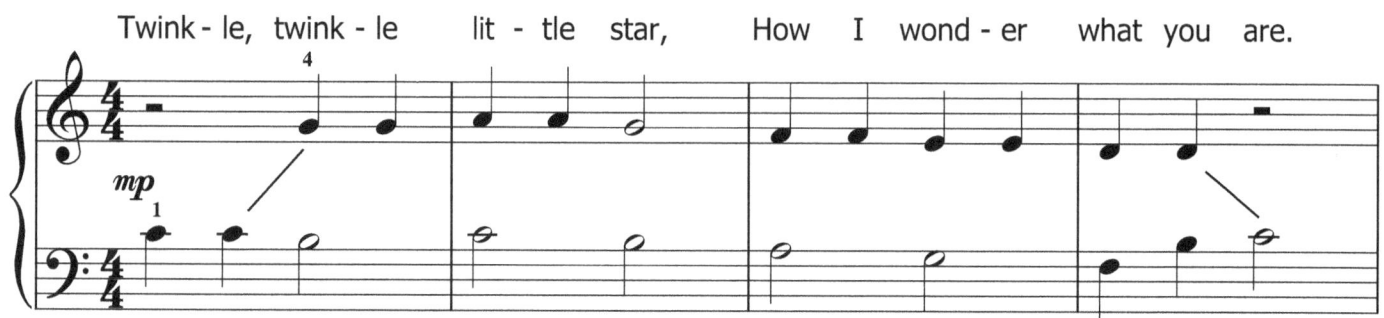

Twink - le, twink - le lit - tle star, How I won - der what you are.

Up a - bove the world so high, Like a dia - mond in the sky,

Twink - le, twink - le lit - tle star, How I won - der what you are.

* The diagonal lines connecting the notes on the two staves, indicate that the melody has travelled into the other stave

Copyright © 2015 Margaret Brandman
International copyright secured APRA/AMCOS. All rights reserved
Photocopying is illegal

I am a Fine Musician

Traditional

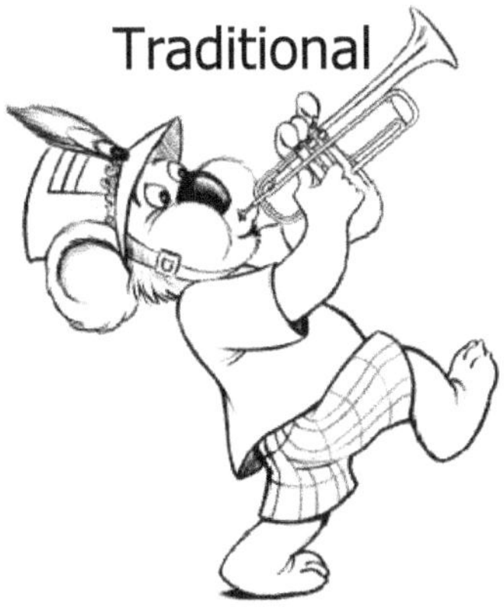

See duet page 1

Arrangement by Margaret Brandman

Moderato

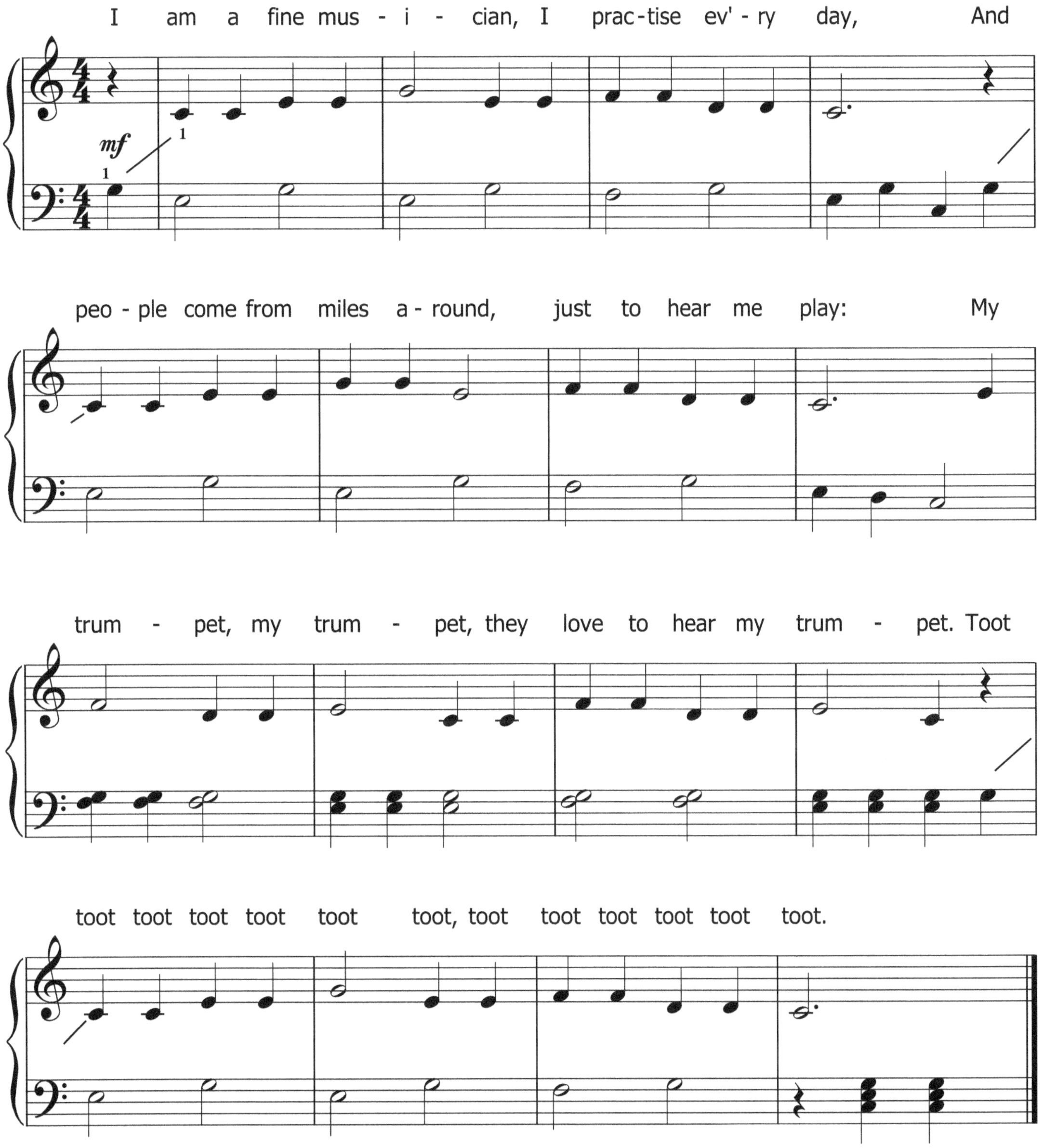

I am a fine mus - i - cian, I prac - tise ev' - ry day, And

peo - ple come from miles a - round, just to hear me play: My

trum - pet, my trum - pet, they love to hear my trum - pet. Toot

toot toot toot toot toot, toot toot toot toot toot toot.

More Finger-Flexers
Amazing Musical Patterns for two-part playing

Finger-Flexer No.4

Lots of *Skip-plus-ones!*

Margaret Brandman

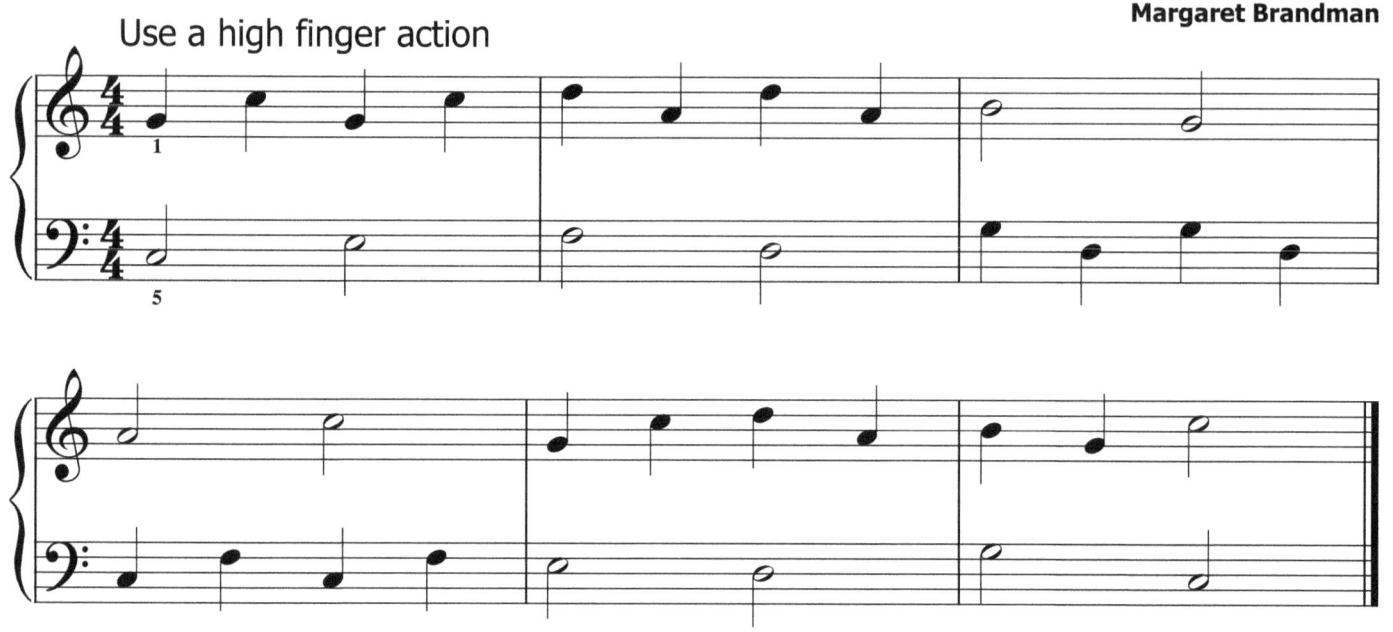

Finger-Flexer No.5

Mostly *Jumps* - but watch out!

Margaret Brandman

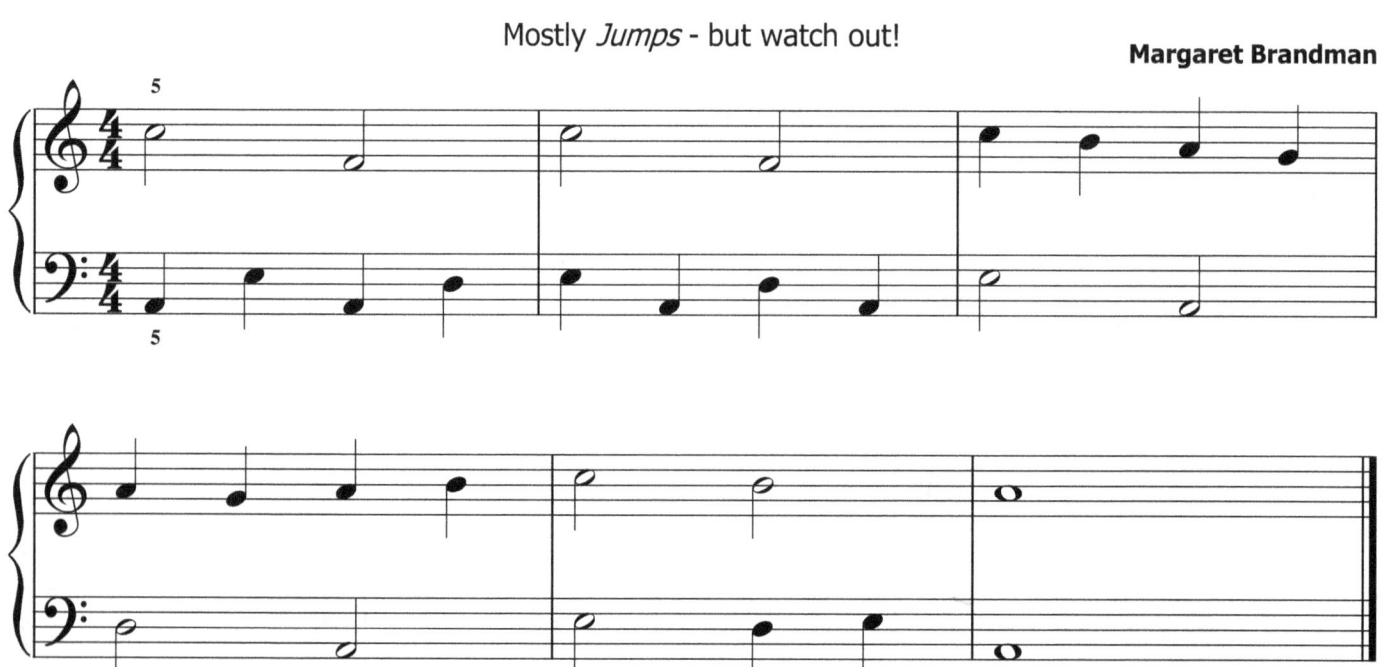

Copyright © 2015 Margaret Brandman
International copyright secured APRA/AMCOS. All rights reserved
Photocopying is illegal

Come Clap Your Hands

See duet page 2

Music and lyrics by Margaret Brandman

Moderato

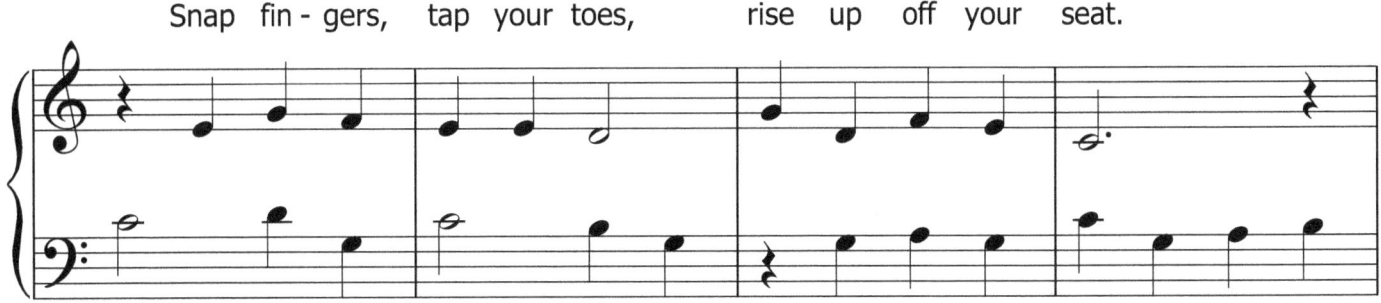

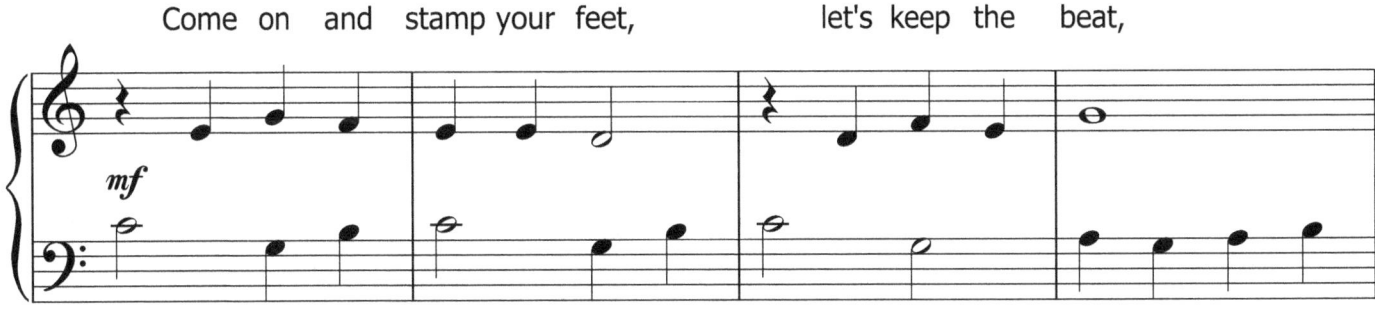

Copyright © 2015 Margaret Brandman
International copyright secured APRA/AMCOS. All rights reserved
Photocopying is illegal

London Bridge is Falling Down

Traditional

See duet page 2

Arrangement by Margaret Brandman

Moderato

Copyright © 2015 Margaret Brandman
International copyright secured APRA/AMCOS. All rights reserved
Photocopying is illegal

Two Fat Gentlemen
Traditional

See duet page 3

Arrangement by Margaret Brandman

Allegretto

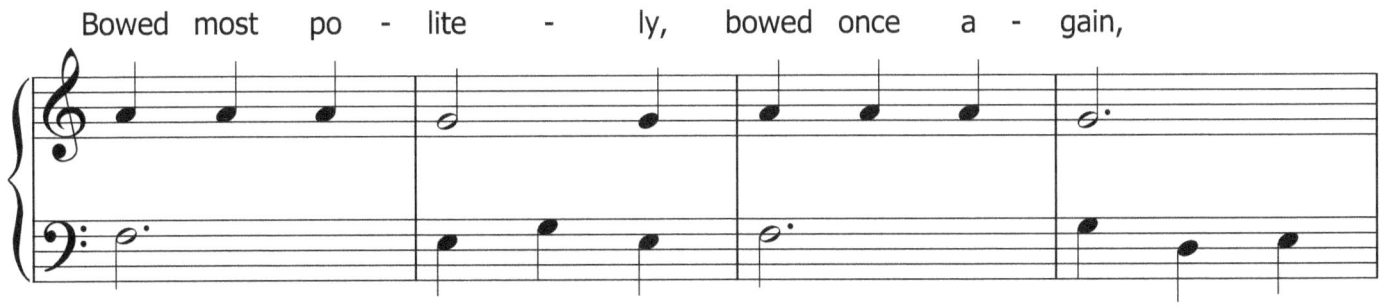

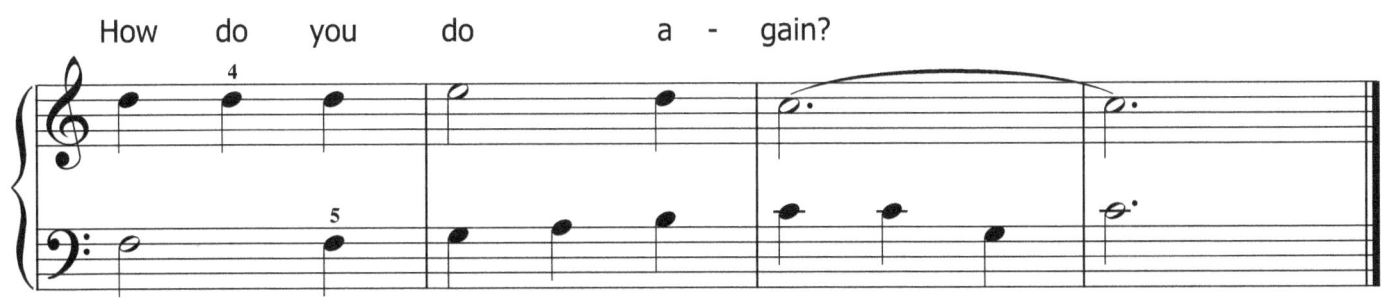

Copyright © 2015 Margaret Brandman
International copyright secured APRA/AMCOS. All rights reserved
Photocopying is illegal

Scooting, Riding, Skating

See duet page 4

Allegretto ♩ = 96

Music and lyrics by Margaret Brandman

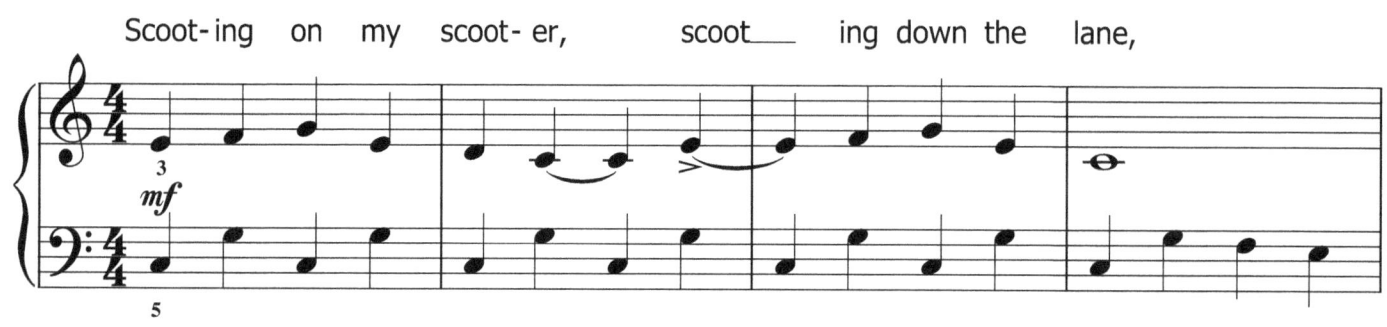

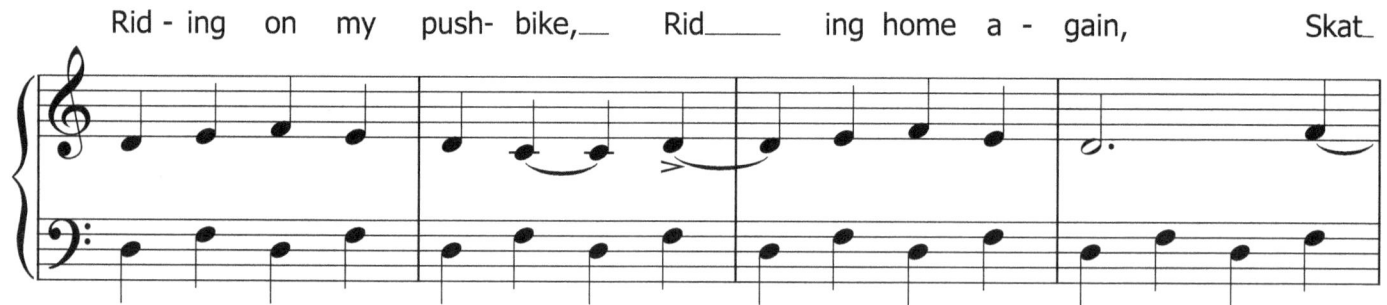

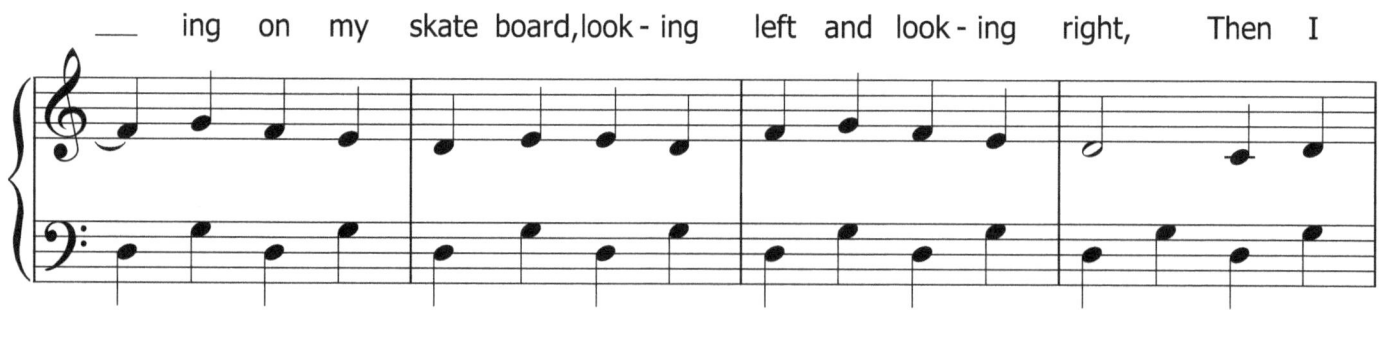

I Love Little Pussy

Traditional

See duet page 3

Arrangement by
Margaret Brandman

Andantino

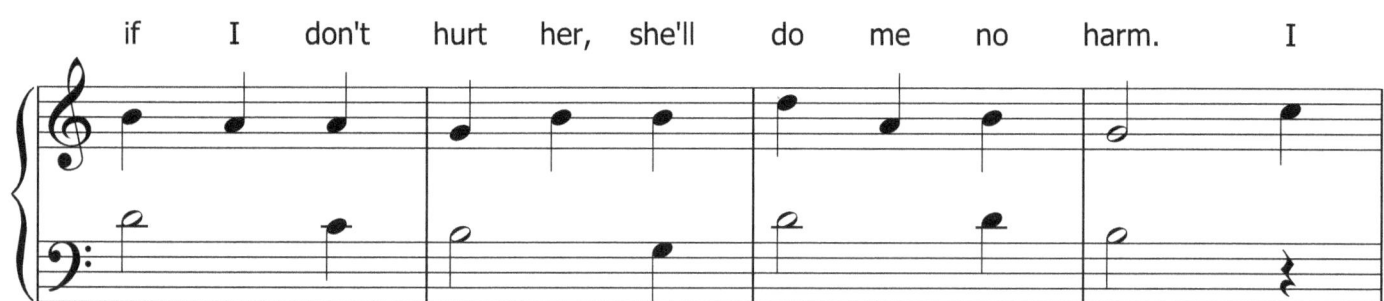

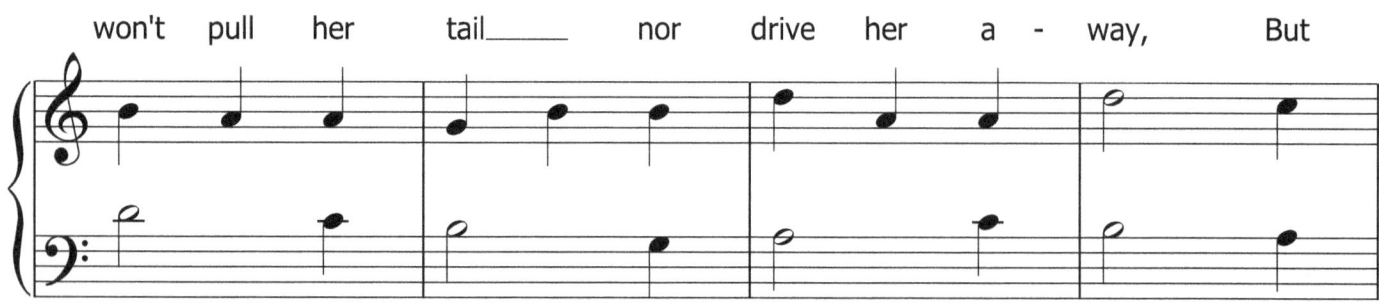

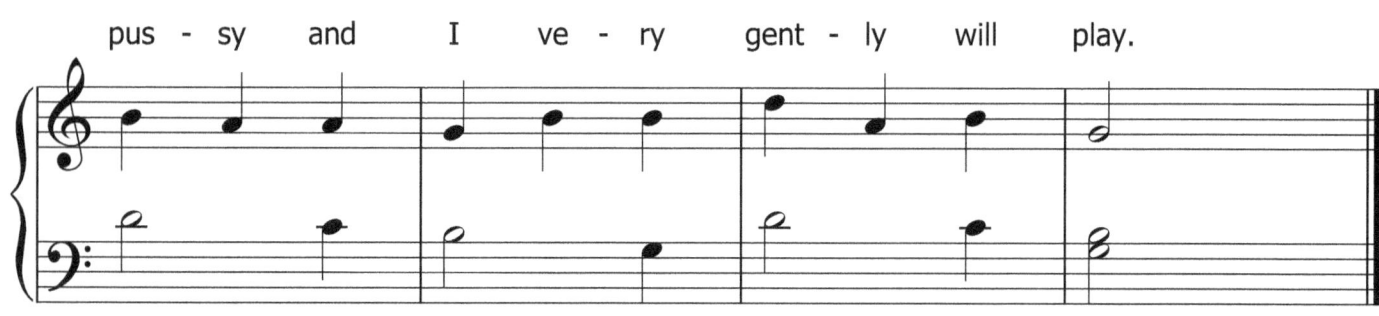

Copyright © 2015 Margaret Brandman
International copyright secured APRA/AMCOS. All rights reserved
Photocopying is illegal

Little Bo Peep

Traditional

See duet page 5

Arrangement by Margaret Brandman

Andante

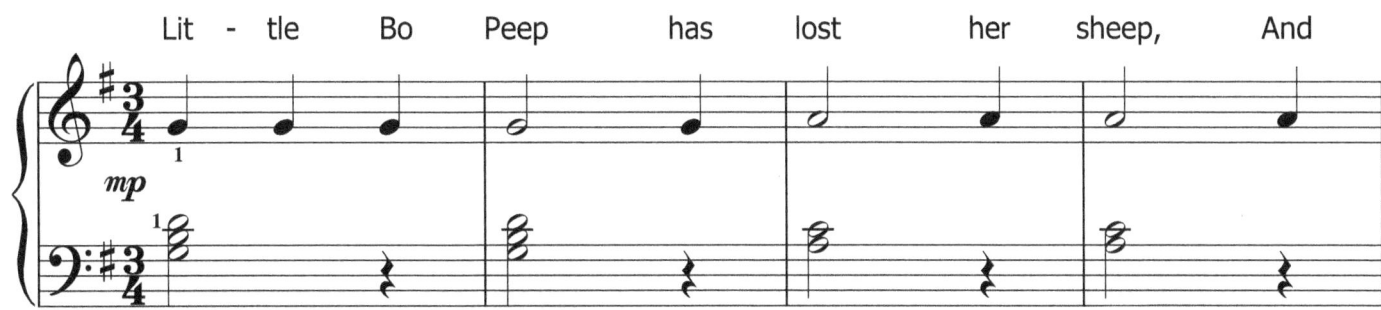

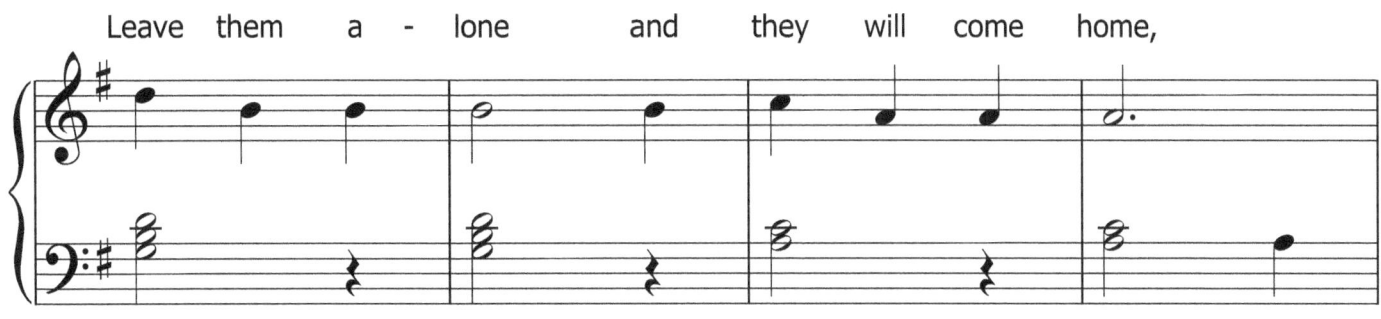

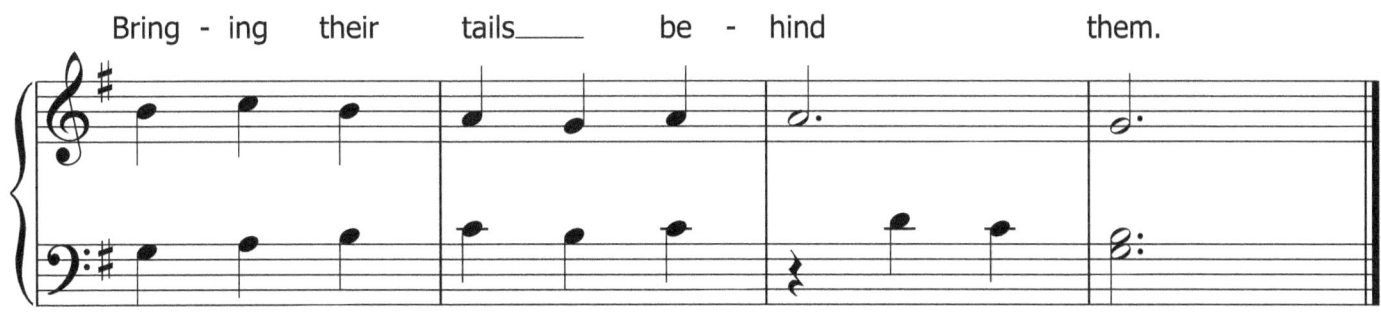

Copyright © 2015 Margaret Brandman
International copyright secured APRA/AMCOS. All rights reserved
Photocopying is illegal

Warm Kitty, Soft Kitty
Traditional English Folk Song

See duet page 5

Arrangement and new lyrics by
Margaret Brandman

Andantino

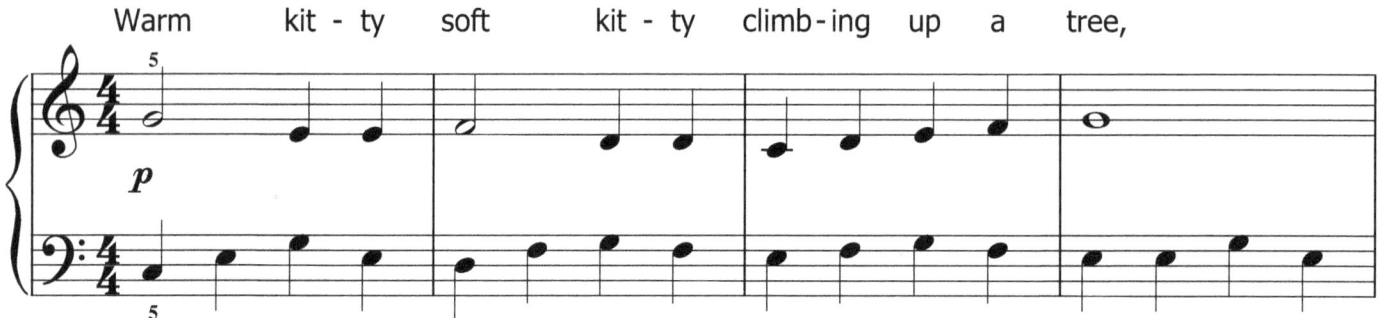

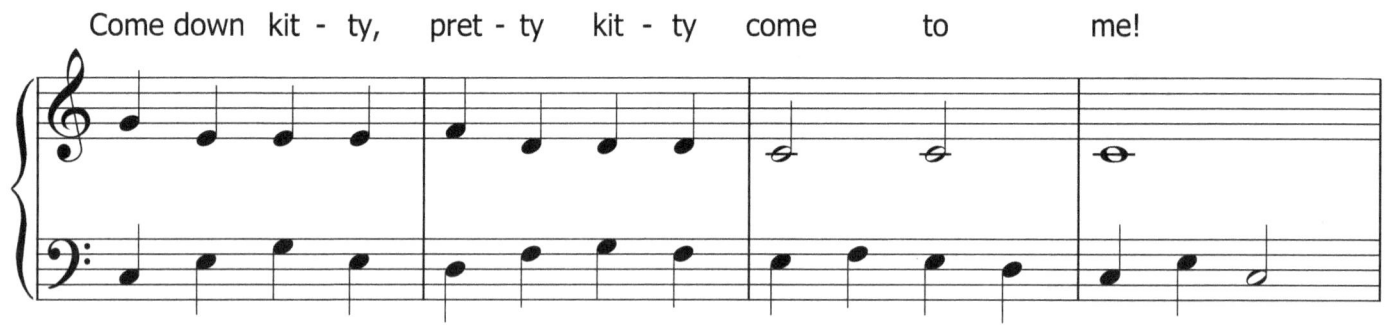

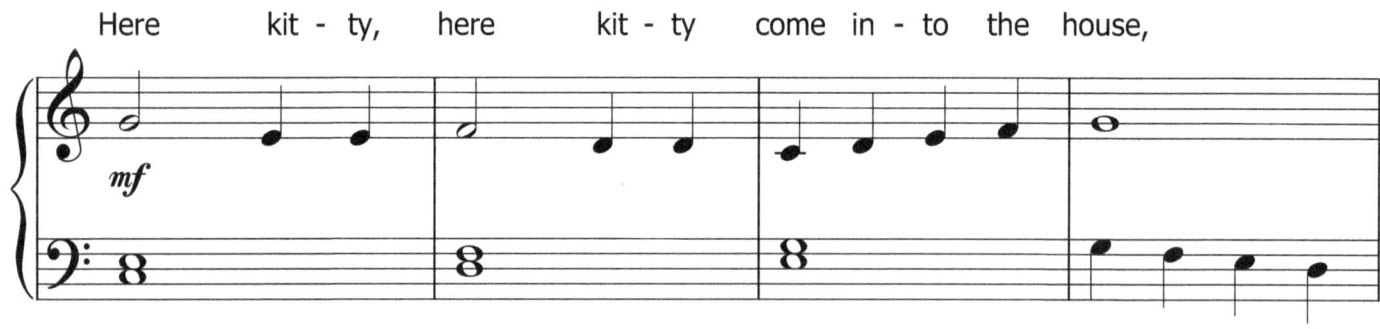

Copyright © 2015 Margaret Brandman
International copyright secured APRA/AMCOS. All rights reserved
Photocopying is illegal

Jingle Jangle

Creativity Corner
Invent your own lyrics for this song.
Here are some words you might like to use:
jingle, jangle, jungle
tingle, tangle, tumble, thimble
ting-a-lingel, sing a little

See duet page 6

Music by
Margaret Brandman

Allegretto

Copyright © 2015 Margaret Brandman
International copyright secured APRA/AMCOS. All rights reserved
Photocopying is illegal

Five Little Ducks

Traditional

See duet page 6

Arrangement by
Margaret Brandman

Moderato

Verse 2: Four little ducks...
Verse 3: Three little ducks...
Verse 4: Two little ducks...

Verse 5:
One little duck went out one day,
Over the hills and far away.
Mother duck said, "Quack, quack, quack, quack"
And none of those little ducks came back.

last verse;
Mother duck went out one day,
Over the hills and far away,
Mother duck said, "Quack. quack, quack, quack"
And *all* of those five little ducks came back.

Copyright © 2015 Margaret Brandman
International copyright secured APRA/AMCOS. All rights reserved
Photocopying is illegal

Mister Frog

Traditional

See duet page 6

Arrangement by Margaret Brandman

Andante

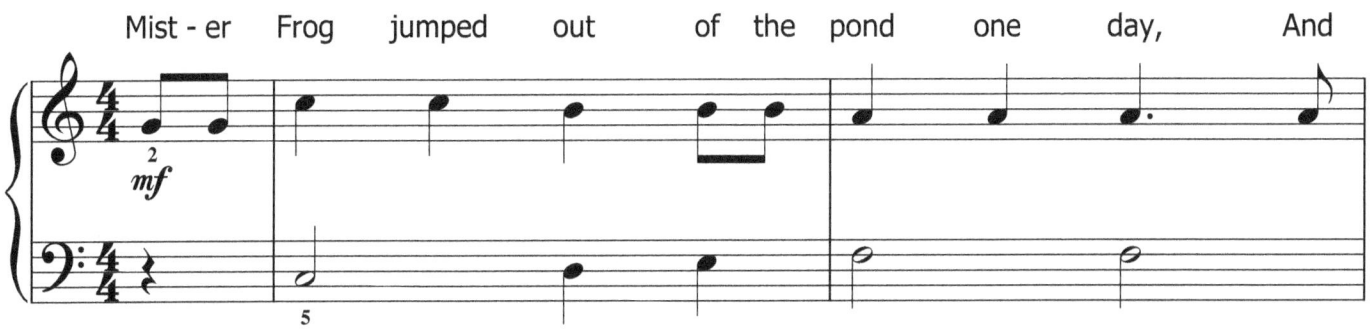

Copyright © 2015 Margaret Brandman
International copyright secured APRA/AMCOS. All rights reserved
Photocopying is illegal

The Jumping Flea

See duet page 7

Music and lyrics by Margaret Brandman

Allegretto

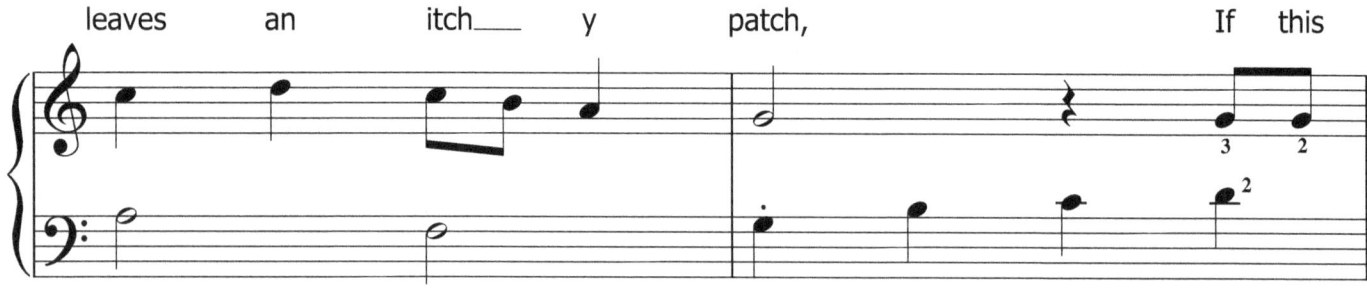

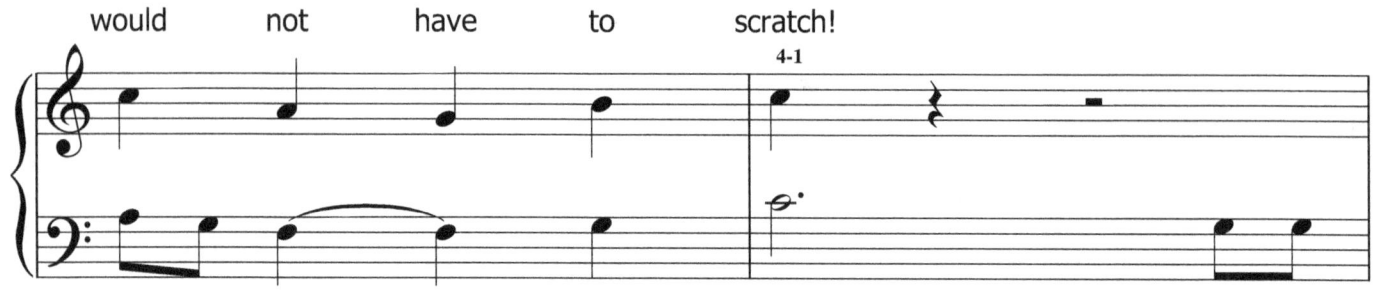

Copyright © 2015 Margaret Brandman
International copyright secured APRA/AMCOS. All rights reserved
Photocopying is illegal

Hush-a-bye, Don't You Cry

Traditional American

See duet page 8

Arrangement by Margaret Brandman

Andante

Hush - a - bye, don't you cry, Go to sleepy lit-tle ba - by.

When you wake, you'll have cake, And all the pret-ty lit-tle hors - es.

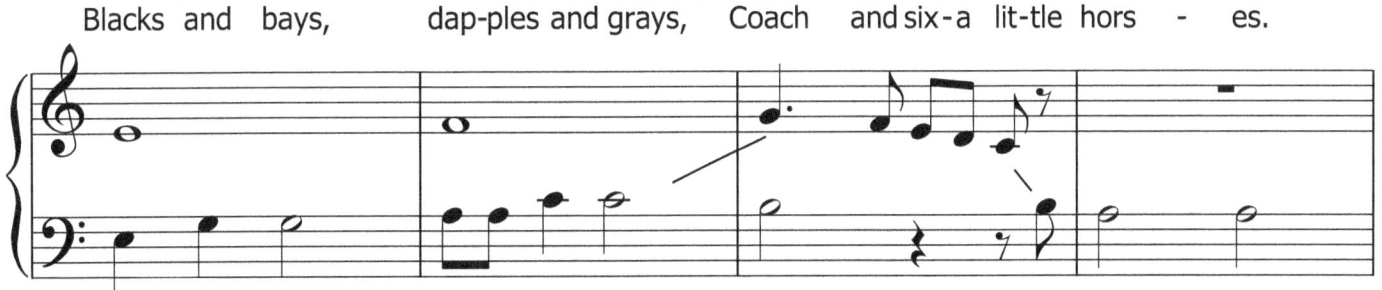

Blacks and bays, dap-ples and grays, Coach and six-a lit-tle hors - es.

Hush a - bye, don't you cry, Go to sleepy lit-tle ba - by.

Copyright © 2015 Margaret Brandman
International copyright secured APRA/AMCOS. All rights reserved
Photocopying is illegal

AWARD CERTIFICATE

This is to certify that

....

has successfully completed

MARGARET BRANDMAN'S

Playing Made Easy

JUNIOR TRAX

and is promoted to

HOT TRAX

....
Date   Teacher

JUNIOR TRAX- DUET PARTS

Twinkle, Twinkle Little Star

I am a Fine Musician

Come Clap Your Hands

Moderato

**Duet part composed by
Margaret Brandman ©2005**

London Bridge is Falling Down

Allegretto

**Duet part composed by
Margaret Brandman ©1999**

Copyright © 2015 Margaret Brandman
International copyright secured APRA/AMCOS. All rights reserved
Photocopying is illegal

Two Fat Gentlemen

I Love Little Pussy

Scooting, Riding, Skating

**Duet part composed by
Margaret Brandman © 2005**

Allegretto

Little Bo Peep

Duet part composed by Margaret Brandman ©1999

Andante

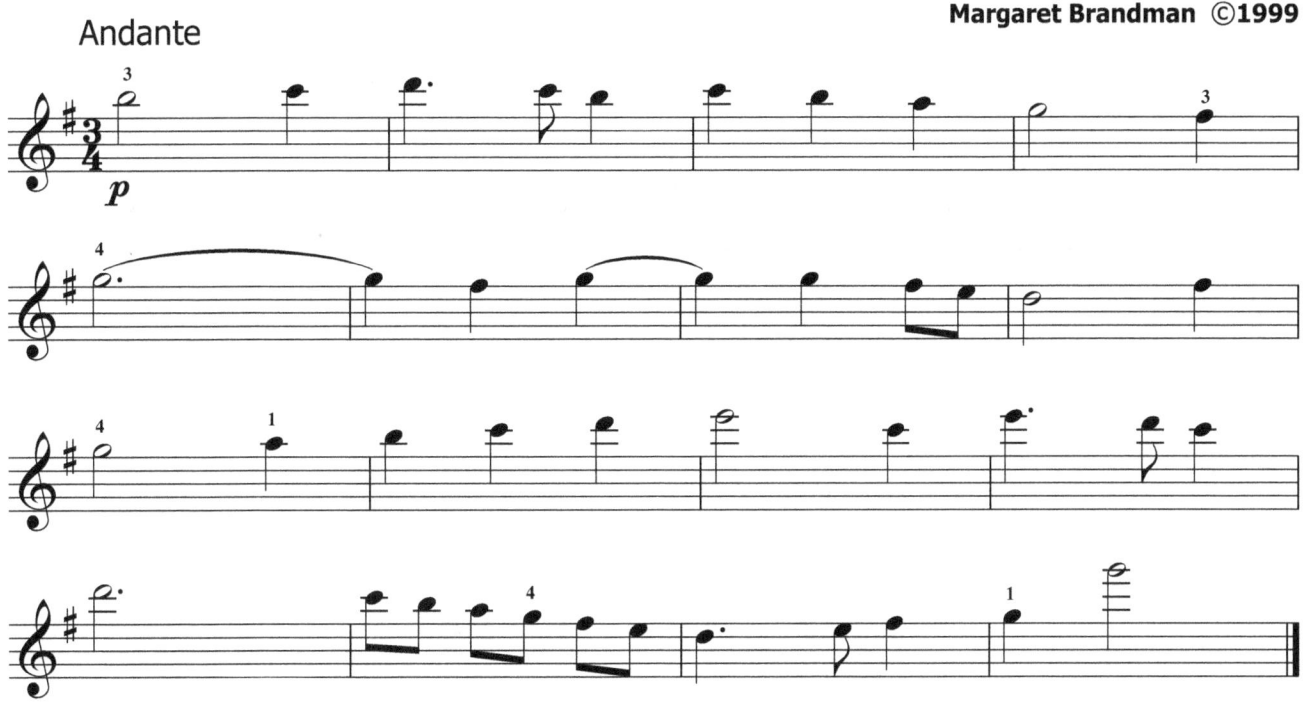

Warm Kitty, Soft Kitty

Duet part composed by Margaret Brandman ©1999

Andantino

Jingle Jangle

Five Little Ducks

Mister Frog

The Jumping Flea

**Duet part composed by
Margaret Brandman ©2005**

Said the Kind Kangaroo

Andantino

**Duet part composed by
Margaret Brandman ©1999**

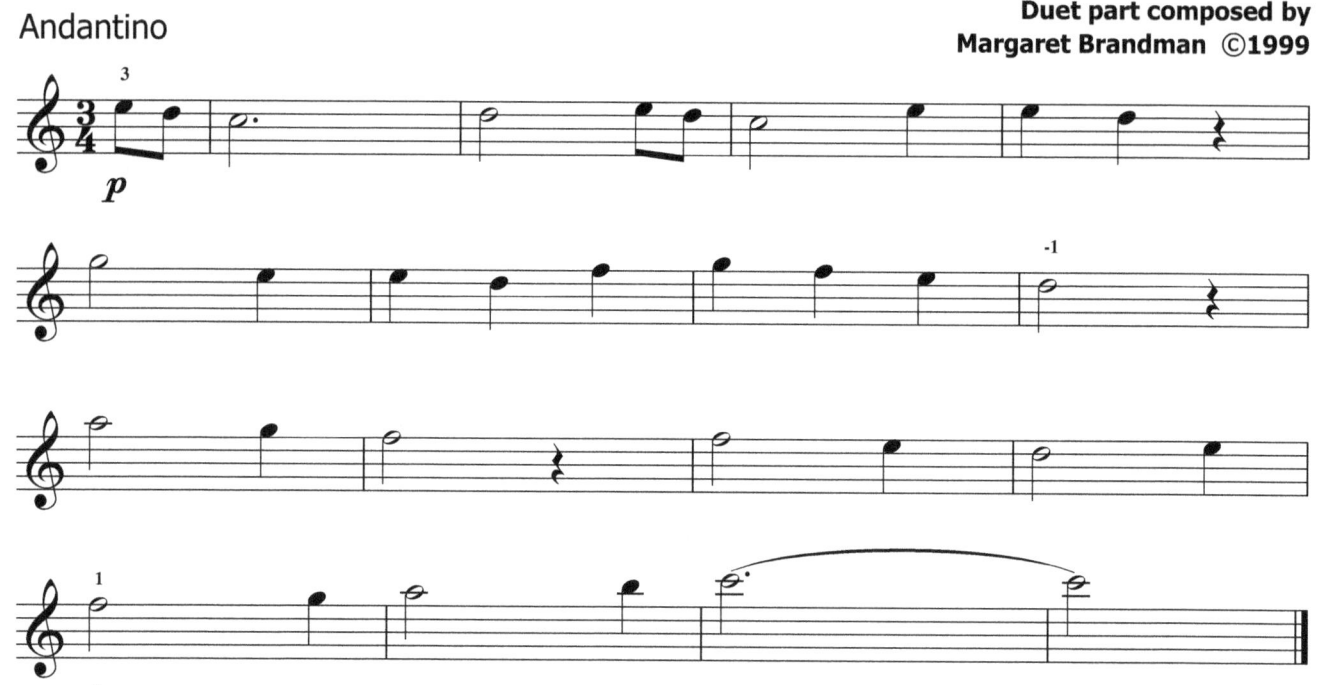

Hush-a-bye, Don't You Cry

Andante

8va throughout

**Duet part composed by
Margaret Brandman ©1999**

Copyright © 2015 Margaret Brandman
International copyright secured APRA/AMCOS. All rights reserved
Photocopying is illegal